Kristen Suzanne's
EASY Raw Vegan Soups

OTHER BOOKS BY KRISTEN SUZANNE

Kristen's Raw: The EASY Way to Get Started & Succeed at the Raw Food Vegan Diet & Lifestyle

Kristen Suzanne's EASY Raw Vegan Entrees

Kristen Suzanne's EASY Raw Vegan Desserts

Kristen Suzanne's EASY Raw Vegan Salads & Dressings

Kristen Suzanne's EASY Raw Vegan Sides & Snacks

Kristen Suzanne's EASY Raw Vegan Smoothies, Juices, Elixirs & Drinks (includes wine drinks!)

Kristen Suzanne's EASY Raw Vegan Holidays

Kristen Suzanne's EASY Raw Vegan Dehydrating

Kristen Suzanne's Ultimate Raw Vegan Hemp Recipes

Kristen Suzanne's Ultimate Raw Vegan Chocolate Recipes

Kristen Suzanne's EASY Raw Vegan Transition Recipes

For details, Raw Food resources, and Kristen's free Raw Food newsletter, please visit:

KristensRaw.com

Kristen Suzanne's

EASY Raw
Vegan Soups

• •

Delicious & Easy Raw Food Recipes
for Hearty, Satisfying, Flavorful Soups

by Kristen Suzanne

*Green
Butterfly
Press*

Scottsdale, Arizona

For information on excerpting, reprinting or licensing portions of this book, please
write to info@greenbutterflypress.com.

Green Butterfly Press
19550 N. Gray Hawk Drive, Suite 1042
Scottsdale, AZ 85255 USA

Library of Congress Control Number: 2008942521
Library of Congress Subject Heading:
1. Cookery (Natural foods) 2. Raw foods

ISBN: 978-0-9817556-4-9

2.0

Contents

• • • • • • • •

1: Easy, High Energy & Versatile 1

2: It's Recipe Time! 5

Arriba Tortilla Soup 7

Rich Pecan-N-Savory Bisque 8

Gourmet Thai Soup 9

Deliciously Basic Green Vegetable Soup 10

Carrot Tart Soup 11

Blueberry Blue Moon Energy Soup 12

Creamy-N-Soft Cauliflower Soup 13

Un-Chicken Noodle Soup 14

Mint Soup 15

Vegetable Stock 16

Creamy Avocado Breeze 17

Creamy Caribbean Soup 18

Bell Pepper Soup Diane 19

Healing Miso Soup 20

Sun-Drenched Sicilian Soup 21

Savory Sweet Mango Soup 22

Kristen Suzanne's Hearty Gazpacho Stew 23

Kristen Suzanne's Famous Creamed
  Carrot Soup 25

Summertime Corn Bisque 26

Sunset Chowder 27

Easy Coconut Curry Soup 28

Lady-in-Red Soup 29

Chinese Spiced Mushroom Bisque 30

Spicy Thyme Bisque 31

Yin-Yang Soup 32

Park-Side Tomato Almond Soup 33

Princess Pink Strawberry Soup 34

Moroccan Rose Gazpacho 35

Nutty Avocado Soup 36

Michigan Cherry Cream of Tomato Soup 37

Deven's Orange-You-Glad Tomato Soup 38

Raw Plant-Based Court Bouillon 39

Secret Garden Ginger Energy Soup 40

Savory On-the-Go Soup 41

Chilled Caribbean Mint Bisque 42

Green Moxie Soup 43

Guacamole Soup 45

Garlic Lemon-Lime Bisque 46

Farmer's Daughter Stew 48

Alkalizing Summer Watermelon Soup 50

Citrus Dill Delight Soup 51

Kitchen Sink Soups 52

Appendix A: Raw Basics   55

Nourishing Rejuvelac................................ 78

Date Paste 80

Crème Fraiche 81

Nut/Seed Milk (regular) 82

Sweet Nut/Seed Cream (thick) 83

Raw Mustard 84

My Basic Raw Mayonnaise 85

Appendix B: Resources   87

Recipe List

● ● ● ● ● ● ● ● ● ●

Alkalizing Summer Watermelon Soup 52

Arriba Tortilla Soup 7

Bell Pepper Soup Diane 20

Blueberry Blue Moon Energy Soup 13

Carrot Tart Soup 12

Chilled Caribbean Mint Bisque 43

Chinese Spiced Mushroom Bisque 31

Citrus Dill Delight Soup 53

Creamy Avocado Breeze 18

Creamy Caribbean Soup 19

Creamy-N-Soft Cauliflower Soup 14

Crème Fraiche 82

Date Paste 81

Deliciously Basic Green Vegetable Soup 11

Deven's Orange-You-Glad Tomato Soup 39

Easy Coconut Curry Soup 29

Farmer's Daughter Stew 50

Garlic Lemon-Lime Bisque 48

Gourmet Thai Soup 10

Green Moxie Soup 44

Guacamole Soup 46

Healing Miso Soup 21

Kitchen Sink Soups 54

Kristen Suzanne's Famous Creamed Carrot Soup . 26

Kristen Suzanne's Hearty Gazpacho Stew 24

Lady-in-Red Soup 30

Michigan Cherry Cream Of Tomato Soup 38

Mint Soup 16

Moroccan Rose Gazpacho 36

My Basic Raw Mayonnaise 86

Nourishing Rejuvelac.. 78

Nut/Seed Milk (regular) 83

Nutty Avocado Soup 37

Park-Side Tomato Almond Soup 34

Princess Pink Strawberry Soup 35

Raw Mustard 85

Raw Plant-Based Court Bouillon 40

Rich Pecan-N-Savory Bisque 9

Savory On-the-Go Soup 42

Savory Sweet Mango Soup 23

Secret Garden Ginger Energy Soup 41

Spicy Thyme Bisque 32

Summertime Corn Bisque 27

Sun-Drenched Sicilian Soup 22

Sunset Chowder 28

Sweet Nut/Seed Cream (thick) 84

Un-Chicken Noodle Soup 15

Vegetable Stock 17

Yin-Yang Soup 33

1
· · ·

Easy, High Energy & Versatile

The health of the people is really the foundation upon which all their happiness and all their powers as a state depend.

BENJAMIN DISRAELI

RAW SOUPS ARE EASY

Raw vegan soups are a mainstay in my life for many reasons. One of which is that they're so easy to make (and I mean really easy!). I can blend up a raw soup in less than 15 minutes, *and* have enough servings to last a few days. This is important for people like myself with a busy, on-the-go lifestyle. There are days when I'm not only extra busy, but I'm also away from my kitchen for hours and hours at a time. It's times like these that I need a quick and nutritious, yet hearty, solution. Raw soups are perfect.

They're easy to transport and consume. When I'm out running errands, I simply drink my raw soup straight out of a glass mason jar.

RAW SOUPS FOR HIGH ENERGY

Another reason that raw vegan soups are a staple in my diet is because they give me bounds and bounds of energy. They're known for giving people energy because they're classified as a "liquid food" or a "blended meal." I make it a point to consume plenty of blended meals in my week and raw soups are great for this. When you consume food in liquefied form, you give your digestive system a rest because it doesn't have to work as hard breaking down all of the food.

But, don't think that because it's "just a soup" that it won't be fulfilling. Nothing could be farther from the truth. Raw soups are hearty and totally satisfying for a couple of different reasons. For one, they're made with super nutrient-dense foods. The other reason is that they're loaded with fiber, which can keep you full for hours.

Soups are also extremely hydrating due to the high water content ingredients. One of the first reasons people become tired and sluggish is because they are dehydrated. Well, if you're consuming lots of fresh Plant Blood (my term for vegetable/fruit juice), smoothies, and raw soups, then you're filling your body with plenty of pure liquids to keep you properly hydrated.

RAW SOUPS ARE VERSATILE

Raw vegan soups have versatility, too. Soup can be an entire meal by itself (I'll drink 2–4 cups when I do this), a snack midday, or complement a meal as an appetizer. They also can be enjoyed all year long. During the hot summer months, I enjoy cold and refreshing raw soups, and in the chilly winter months I simply warm my raw soups up a bit to give me that cozy comfy feeling (without cooking them... details below).

WARM OR COLD?—A NOTE ON WARMING SOUPS

Because "Raw" means uncooked, that often means cold or room-temperature food. Sometimes it's hard for people to get used to drinking cold soups, especially in the chilly winter months. Here are many ways that can help.

1. Use your dehydrator to warm the soup. This is the recommended option, as it's the best and safest way to warm your soup. I explain it as "safest" because I'm referring to the nutrients and enzymes. By warming your raw soup in the dehydrator with the following instructions, you can be sure that you're not harming the integrity of the nutrients.

    To warm your raw soup this way, set the soup in your dehydrator (either in a glass mason jar or a glass bowl) for 1–2 hours at 130–140 degrees. Then, enjoy.

    If you're in the market for a dehydrator, I strongly recommend Excalibur dehydrators. For details about where to find them, visit KristensRaw.com/store.

2. Another great option to warm the soup is by using your blender. Many high-powered blenders will actually warm your soup to a hot serving temperature; hence, you have to be careful that you don't get it to that point. However, you can blend your soup for about 1–2 minutes on high speed to help warm your soup. This method is best when warming a soup that doesn't have avocado in it (or the texture gets too "whipped"). However, if you want to use your blender to warm a recipe with avocado in it, then blend the soup to your desired temperature, and then add the avocado last. If you're like me and you keep your avocados

on your counter top, then it'll be room temperature when adding it to your "already" blended soup, therefore not cooling the temperature much at all by adding the avocado last.

3. Just because you are eating lots of raw food doesn't mean you have to totally stop using your stove. You can warm your soup using your stove on the lowest setting. As long as you can use your finger to stir the soup, without it feeling too hot, then the temperature is okay without compromising the enzymes or nutrient profile.

4. If your raw soup has been in the refrigerator, it's a simple solution to let the soup sit at room temperature before eating. This does take time though, so plan ahead.

5. One of my favorite solutions to warming raw vegan soup is by adding warming spices to it. They're like magic because they don't actually warm the soup's temperature per se, but they do give *you* a warm sensation when eating it. See? That's like magic! The following are great ways to do this: fresh ginger, cayenne, hot peppers (habanero—super hot! or red Serrano are a couple examples that I like to use), horseradish, wasabi, and/or garlic. It doesn't matter how cold a soup is, these can help you think it's actually quite warm because of their stimulating nature. In fact, you might just need a glass of cold water ready to drink in case it warms you too much.

2
· · ·

It's Recipe Time!

Within each of us lies the power of our consent to health and sickness, to riches and poverty, to freedom and to slavery. It is we who control these, and not another.

RICHARD BACH

The following recipes are filled with delicious nutrition. They are sure to make your cells sing for joy. Raw soups can be used as meals, snacks, or appetizers. Enjoy!

PHOTOS OF RECIPES AVAILABLE AT:

KristensRaw.com/photos

The following soups made from recipes in this book have been photographed. See KristensRaw.com/photos for pretty pictures of:

- Arriba Tortilla Soup
- Alkalizing Summer Watermelon Soup
- Blueberry Blue Moon Energy Soup
- Creamy-n-Soft Cauliflower Soup
- Healing Miso Soup

- Kristen Suzanne's Famous Creamed Carrot Soup
- Lady-in-Red Soup
- Princess Pink Strawberry Soup
- Savory On-the-Go Soup
- Garlic Lemon-Lime Bisque
- Citrus Dill Delight Soup

I always like to get feedback on my photographs! (In addition to hearing your stories about my recipes too!) If you visit the site, please let me know your favorites by writing to me at:

Kristen@KristensRaw.com

Arriba Tortilla Soup

See photo at KristensRaw.com/photos.

Yield 4 cups

This soup is vibrant and gorgeous! If you're a fan of Mexican food, then this soup is right up your alley. I love the fiery kick to it… just enough to bring you back begging for more.

I like to really "play" when I'm in the kitchen, so when I make this soup, I wear my gigantic sombrero (it cracks my husband up).

1 cup water

1 ½ cups yellow bell pepper, chopped

2 cups yellow zucchini, chopped

1 cup butternut squash, peeled, seeded and chopped

1 soft date, pitted

1 clove garlic

1 green onion (white part only)

2 tablespoons fresh lime juice

2 ½ teaspoons Mexican seasoning

¾ teaspoon cumin

½ teaspoon Himalayan crystal salt, more to taste

¼ teaspoon cayenne pepper

½ cup raw olive oil

Blend all of the ingredients, except for the raw olive oil, until very smooth. This could take a minute so that the butternut squash gets thoroughly blended. Then, while the blender is running, slowly add the raw olive oil.

Rich Pecan-N-Savory Bisque

Yield 4 servings

This bisque is so rich and creamy, making it perfect on a chilly fall day. I love eating it with a side dish of sliced apples. Pecans have a great reputation because they are loaded with nutrients such as vitamin E, potassium, phytosterols, heart-healthy mono-unsaturated fats, and fiber.

> 2 ½ cups water
>
> 1 cup raw pecans
>
> 1 large clove garlic
>
> 2 tablespoons fresh lemon juice
>
> 1 tablespoon raw agave nectar
>
> 1 tablespoon tamari, wheat-free
>
> 1 teaspoon Himalayan crystal salt
>
> ½ teaspoon black pepper
>
> pinch cinnamon
>
> ½ avocado, pitted and peeled
>
> ¾ cup raw olive oil or hemp oil
>
> chopped scallions to garnish

Blend the water and nuts until smooth. Add the rest of the ingredients, except the avocado, raw olive oil, and scallions, and blend. Add the avocado and blend until creamy. While blending on low speed, slowly add the raw olive oil until it is well incorporated. Garnish with chopped scallions.

Gourmet Thai Soup

Yield 5–6 cups

This soup's nutrient profile has an impressive resume from the ginger to the coconut to the zucchini to the curry powder to the cinnamon and more.

4 cups zucchini, peeled and chopped

1 ½ cups water

1 cup young Thai coconut water

⅓ cup young Thai coconut meat

½ cup fresh lime juice

2 tablespoons powdered ginger

1 ½ tablespoons fresh ginger, peeled and minced

1 tablespoon garlic powder

1 tablespoon Himalayan crystal salt

1 tablespoon raw agave nectar

2 teaspoons curry powder

¾ teaspoon cardamom

¼ teaspoon cinnamon

dash allspice powder

smidge white pepper

dash cayenne pepper, optional

½ cup coconut oil

Blend all of the ingredients, except the coconut oil. While the blender is running on low, slowly add the coconut oil.

Deliciously Basic Green Vegetable Soup

Yield 4–5 servings

It's important to have a staple green vegetable soup in your library of recipes. Feel free to add different herbs and vegetables to put your own spin on it.

One of the reasons I love spinach is because it's a notable source of vitamin K, which is known for helping you build stronger bones. And, I'm sure you've heard before that spinach is a great source of iron, but what you might not know is that it's better assimilated in your body when it's in the presence of vitamin C (found in the fresh lime juice).

> 2 ½ cups water
>
> 1 cup romaine, chopped
>
> 1 cup spinach, packed
>
> 3 tablespoons fresh lime juice
>
> ½ teaspoon kelp, or more to taste
>
> ½ teaspoon Himalayan crystal salt, or more to taste
>
> 1 banana, peeled and chopped
>
> 1 avocado, pitted and peeled
>
> 2 tablespoons fresh basil, chopped or 2 teaspoons dried
>
> 2 tablespoons green onions, chopped

Blend all of the ingredients, except the avocado, basil and green onions. Add the avocado and blend until smooth and creamy. Pulse in the basil and green onions.

Carrot Tart Soup

Yield 2 servings

Even though there are only a handful of ingredients in this easy soup, they pack a nutritional punch.

Walnuts are known as brain food (kind of neat that they actually look like mini-brains, eh?) because of their omega-3 content. The carrots arm your body with plenty of nutrients as well, including a high level of carotenoids, which are known to help fight various types of cancer.

> ⅓ cup raw walnuts, ground
> Juice of whole pink grapefruit
> 3 medium carrots, chopped
> ⅓ cup raw olive oil
> 2 tablespoons water
> pinch Himalayan crystal salt, or more to taste
> pinch black pepper

Grind the walnuts to a fine grind in a dry blender or food processor, fitted with the "S" blade. Add the remaining ingredients and blend until smooth.

Blueberry Blue Moon Energy Soup

See photo at KristensRaw.com/photos.

Yield approximately 2 ½ cups

I love serving this soup to my guests because of the color (so vibrant, impressive, and fun!). Blueberries pack a gorgeous and highly nutritious punch in this delicious soup.

It's a great soup to have for lunch, or as a super healthy, high-energy snack! I also love drinking it as a smoothie in the morning or right before a workout!

> 1 cup young Thai coconut water
>
> 1 banana, peeled and chopped
>
> 1 cup blueberries
>
> 1 teaspoon fresh lemon juice
>
> smidge Himalayan crystal salt

Blend all of the ingredients briefly in a blender.

Creamy-N-Soft Cauliflower Soup

See photo at KristensRaw.com/photos.

Yield approximately 3 cups

For those of you who are not fans of cauliflower, I have the soup for you! This recipe is awesome. I named it "Creamy-n-Soft Cauliflower Soup" because the texture is velvety smooth and creamy, while the flavor is delicate and soft... a delectable combination.

Even though we Raw Fooders like to brag about our vibrant color dishes that are the colors of the rainbow, it's important to remember that fresh white produce also has many nutritional properties essential for optimal health. Step in: Cauliflower. This amazing member of the cabbage family contains indoles and sulforaphane, which basically means that consumption of cauliflower can help you fight and/or prevent cancer.

1 cup water
2 cups cauliflower, chopped
⅔ cup pine nuts
2 teaspoons onion powder
3 tablespoons fresh lemon juice
1 teaspoon raw agave nectar
pinch white pepper
Himalayan crystal salt, to taste

Place the pine nuts in a bowl with enough water to cover by about an inch. Let them soak on your countertop for about an hour. Drain off the water and give them a quick rinse. Blend all of the ingredients until velvety smooth.

Un-Chicken Noodle Soup

Yield 4 servings

This soup takes a tiny bit of effort because it requires juicing some of the ingredients, but the reward of tasting it afterward is totally worth it!

- ½ cup fresh carrot juice
- 1 cup fresh celery juice
- ¾ cup fresh daikon radish juice
- 1 ½ cups water
- 2 cucumbers, peeled and chopped
- 2 tablespoons fresh lemon juice
- 1 teaspoon poultry seasoning
- 1 teaspoon onion powder
- ½ teaspoon cumin
- ½ teaspoon Himalayan crystal salt, or more to taste
- ½ cup red bell pepper, seeded and diced
- ½ cup carrot, diced
- 1 avocado, pitted, peeled, and diced
- 1–2 zucchini, spiralized

Using a juicer, juice the carrots, celery and daikon radish. Transfer the juice to a blender with the water, cucumbers, lemon juice, poultry seasoning, onion powder, cumin, and salt. Blend thoroughly. Stir in the diced veggies and spiralized zucchini noodles.

Mint Soup

This is an easy to make, nice, and mellow, creamy soup. I am particularly fond of it in the summer because mint gives a nice cooling quality to it. For this reason, it's not a soup that I would want to warm up.

> 1 ½ cups Nut/Seed Milk, sweetened to taste* (see recipe, Appendix A)
>
> 1 cucumber, peeled and chopped
>
> 1 tablespoon fresh lemon juice
>
> ½ teaspoon cumin seeds
>
> ½ teaspoon Himalayan crystal salt
>
> 2–3 tablespoons fresh mint, minced & packed

Blend the nut milk, cucumber, lemon juice, cumin seeds, and salt until creamy. Pulse in the fresh mint.

* This soup recipe is best if you're using nut milk that you made with a sweetener, such as dates or agave.

Vegetable Stock

Yield approximately 1 quart

Use this recipe whenever a vegetable stock (or water) is called for in a soup. Or, use as is and add chopped veggies and seasoning to it to make a soup of your own creation.

1 medium tomato

1 cup carrot, chopped

½ cup celery, chopped

2 tablespoons leek, white part only, chopped

1 tablespoon shallot, chopped

1 ½ tablespoons scallions, chopped

4 cups water

Place the tomato, carrot, celery, leek, shallot, scallions and 2 cups of the water in a blender, and blend until the mixture is pureed. Strain, with a nut milk bag, into a container and add the remaining water.

Creamy Avocado Breeze

Yield 3 cups

This soup has a nice play between texture and flavor. The light flavors balance wonderfully with the avocado, which lends a heavier experience. Not only is avocado rich in texture, but it also is rich in nutrients. It's filled with a whopping 9 grams of dietary fiber (sometimes more!), plus plenty of B-vitamins, including folic acid—making this an excellent choice of fruit for pregnant ladies.

 1 ½ cups water
 1 cucumber, peeled and chopped
 ¼ cup fresh lime juice
 2 teaspoons Chinese 5-Spice
 ½ teaspoon onion powder
 ½ teaspoon powdered ginger
 ½ teaspoon Himalayan crystal salt
 dash cayenne pepper
 1 avocado, pitted and peeled
 1 ½ scallions, chopped

Blend all of the ingredients, except the avocado and scallions. Add the avocado and blend until creamy. Pulse in the scallions.

Creamy Caribbean Soup

Yield 4 servings

This is a perfect cold and refreshing soup to take to the beach in a cooler. And, if you're not going to the beach, make the soup anyway and with each sip, your mind will take you there.

> ¾ cup water
>
> 1 pineapple, peeled, cored, and chopped
>
> 2 ripe mangos, peeled and pitted
>
> 1 tablespoon fresh orange zest
>
> 1 teaspoon rum extract, or more to taste
>
> 1 cup Nut/Seed Milk (see recipe, Appendix A)

In a blender, blend the water, pineapple and mangoes until creamy. Add the orange zest, rum extract, and nut milk and blend.

Bell Pepper Soup Diane

Yield 6 cups

This bisque is so good. All of my clients love it, especially Diane, who I had in mind when I created it. Red bell peppers are an excellent source of vitamin C and also contain a nice amount of vitamin A, beta-carotene, and B-vitamins.

2 ½ cups water

2 red, orange, or yellow bell peppers, seeded and chopped

2 cucumbers, peeled and chopped

2 tablespoons red onion or 2 green onions, chopped

½ cup raw olive oil or flax oil

3 tablespoons fresh lemon juice

2 teaspoons Himalayan crystal salt

1 large clove garlic

1 ½ teaspoons caraway seeds

1 teaspoon Italian seasoning

dash black pepper

Blend all of the ingredients in a blender until creamy.

Healing Miso Soup

See photo at KristensRaw.com/photos.

Yield approximately 3 cups

Years ago, when I worked in Hong Kong (long before I was vegan, let alone Raw), I became very ill during one of my visits. As a result, I was fed bowl after bowl of miso soup because it's thought to be healing. Well, I did get better.

> 1 ½ cups warm water
>
> 1 ⅔ cups zucchini, chopped
>
> 2 tablespoons light miso
>
> 1 tablespoon Dandelion Leek Miso*
>
> 2 tablespoons raw olive oil
>
> 1 avocado, pitted, peeled, and diced

Blend the warm water, zucchini, and both flavors of miso until creamy. I love serving this soup slightly warm for the ultimate experience. Therefore, part of the process is using warm water and the other part is blending the ingredients for over a minute, because blending helps warm the soup.

While the blender is running, add the oil. Then, add half of the diced avocado to the blender and continue blending until creamy. Transfer to serving bowl(s) and stir in the remaining diced avocado. Garnish with sprouts, if desired.

* See Appendix B: Resources

Sun-Drenched Sicilian Soup

Yield 4–5 servings

This soup is delicious with the fragrant herbs.

½ cup sun-dried tomatoes

3 tomatoes, chopped

1 zucchini, chopped

3 tablespoons fresh fennel bulb, minced

⅓ cup raw olive oil

1 tablespoon fresh rosemary leaves, or 1 teaspoon dried

1 teaspoon apple cider vinegar

1 teaspoon Himalayan crystal salt, or more to taste

1–2 cloves garlic

2 tablespoons fresh basil, minced, or 2 teaspoons dried

1 tablespoon fresh oregano or 1 teaspoon dried

⅛ teaspoon cinnamon

pinch black pepper

Place the sun-dried tomatoes in a bowl with enough water to cover them by about a half inch. Let them soak on your countertop for an hour. Drain off the water. Blend all of the ingredients in a blender until creamy.

Savory Sweet Mango Soup

Yield 4–5 cups

This is sunshine in a cup. I can't help but smile from ear to ear with each sip. In India, the mango tree is revered as a sacred tree and it's a symbol of love. The fragrant flesh is a gorgeous and vibrant golden orange color and extremely juicy. Fresh mango is filled with Vitamins C, A, K, and D, as well as calcium, magnesium, phosphorus, fiber, and more.

1 ¼ cups water

2–3 mangos, peeled, seeded, and chopped

2 zucchini, peeled and chopped

2 tablespoons fresh lime juice

1–2 cloves garlic

2 tablespoons raw olive oil

1 teaspoon Himalayan crystal salt

pinch cayenne pepper

¼ cup cilantro leaves, chopped

Blend all of the ingredients, except the cilantro, in a blender until smooth and creamy. Add the chopped cilantro and pulse to mix briefly. Enjoy this scrumptious and refreshing soup.

Kristen Suzanne's Hearty Gazpacho Stew

Yield 4–5 servings

This is a nutritious, hearty, and fresh soup that I am particularly fond of during the summer.

The Base

   ½ cup sun-dried tomatoes

   2 tomatoes, chopped

   2 zucchini, peeled and chopped

   ½ cup water

   ¼ cup raw olive oil

   2 cloves garlic

   1 tablespoon raw agave nectar

   ⅓ cup fresh lemon juice

   1 teaspoon Himalayan crystal salt

   pinch cayenne pepper

   ½ cup fresh basil leaves, packed, chopped

   1 tablespoon fresh sage, chopped, or 1 teaspoon dried

The Hearty Ingredients

   1 orange or yellow bell pepper, seeded and diced

   2 stalks celery, diced

   2 medium carrots, diced

   2 tablespoons shallots, minced

   ¼ cup pine nuts

   3 tablespoons raisins

Place the sun-dried tomatoes in a bowl with enough water to cover them by about a half inch. Let them soak on your countertop for 15-30 minutes. Drain off the water and sliver them. Blend all of the ingredients together for the soup base. Prepare the hearty ingredients and stir them into the soup base.

Kristen Suzanne's Famous Creamed Carrot Soup

See photo on cover and at KristensRaw.com/photos.

Yield approximately 4 cups

This is one of my most requested soups from clients. It's creamy, delicious, and extra nutritious.

> 2 cups fresh carrot juice
>
> ½ cup water
>
> 3 tablespoons fresh lemon juice
>
> 1 clove garlic
>
> 1 ½ teaspoons Himalayan crystal salt
>
> 1 teaspoon cumin
>
> 1 teaspoon garlic powder
>
> ⅛ teaspoon cayenne pepper
>
> dash cinnamon
>
> 2 avocados, pitted and peeled
>
> Chopped vegetables (any assortment)—optional

Blend all of the ingredients, except the avocado and chopped vegetables. Add the avocado and blend until smooth and creamy. Stir in the chopped vegetables and serve.

Variations:

- Add ¼ cup raisins after blending.
- Garnish with chopped scallions or sprouts.

Summertime Corn Bisque

Yield 3–4 cups

Summer is great because you can get your hands on fresh, sweet corn. So, to make sure I have corn in the winter months, without resorting to blanched, frozen commercial corn, I buy plenty of fresh organic corn in the summer, cut it off of the cob and freeze it myself with my Food Saver™.

2 cups fresh corn, cut from the cob (or 2 cups frozen corn)

1 cup water

3 tablespoons raw almond butter or 2 tablespoons raw hemp seed butter

1–2 tablespoons shallot, minced

2 teaspoons lemon juice

1 teaspoon Himalayan crystal salt

¾ teaspoon poultry seasoning

½ teaspoon cumin

¼ teaspoon Mexican seasoning

dash black pepper

dash cayenne pepper

2 stalks celery, chopped

Blend all of the ingredients, except the celery, in a blender until smooth and creamy. Stir in the chopped celery.

Sunset Chowder

Yield 2 cups

This beautiful chowder is creamy and reminds me of a relaxing California ocean sunset. This soup is even more delicious if you warm it in the dehydrator.

> 1 cup raw cashews (or pine nuts)
>
> ½ cup water
>
> 1 red bell pepper, seeded and chopped
>
> ½ zucchini, peeled and chopped
>
> 2 tablespoons fresh lemon juice
>
> 1 clove garlic
>
> 1 Serrano red pepper, seeded and chopped
>
> ¼ inch fresh ginger, peeled and grated
>
> 1 ½ teaspoons dulse leaves
>
> ½ teaspoon Himalayan crystal salt

Place the cashews in a bowl with enough water to cover by about an inch. Let them soak on your countertop for 1 hour. Drain off the water and give them a quick rinse. Blend all of the ingredients together in a blender until nice and creamy.

Easy Coconut Curry Soup

Yield 2–3 servings

Here is an easy and terrific Thai flavored soup that is full of delicious nutrition.

    1 young Thai coconut, meat and water

    3 medium carrots, chopped

    1 apple, cored and chopped

    1 ½ tablespoons red onion, chopped

    1 tablespoon fresh orange juice

    1 tablespoon fresh lime juice

    1 tablespoon curry powder

    2 tablespoons coconut oil

    2 teaspoons fresh ginger, peeled, minced or ½ teaspoon
        ground

    1 teaspoon Himalayan crystal salt

    pinch cayenne pepper

Blend all of the ingredients until smooth.

Lady-in-Red Soup

See photo at KristensRaw.com/photos.

Yield approximately 2 cups

I love using different spices in my dishes and garam masala is definitely one of them. Garam masala is a blend of common Indian spices, whose literal meaning is "hot (or warm) spice." This beautiful soup has a calming way about it, as it gently stirs warmth inside you.

> 2 medium tomatoes, chopped
> ½ cup beet, chopped
> 2 tablespoons raw olive oil
> 1 soft date, pitted
> 1 teaspoon apple cider vinegar
> 1 teaspoon garam masala
> ½ teaspoon orange blossom water
> ¼ teaspoon Himalayan crystal salt, or more to taste
> pinch white pepper

Blend all of the ingredients in a blender until smooth and creamy.

Variation:

- Stir in 2 tablespoons of both pine nuts and dried cherries (or raisins) after blending.

Chinese Spiced Mushroom Bisque

Yield 4 cups

Mushrooms have B-vitamins, and cremini mushrooms in particular also have selenium, copper, zinc, and phosphorus.

> **2 cups water**
>
> **4 cups cremini or portabella mushrooms**
>
> **¼ cup raw tahini**
>
> **¼ cup raw olive oil**
>
> **3 tablespoons fresh lemon juice**
>
> **2 tablespoons tamari, wheat-free**
>
> **2 tablespoons fresh basil, chopped**
>
> **1 ¼ teaspoons Chinese 5-Spice powder**
>
> **1 teaspoon onion powder**
>
> **black pepper, to taste**

Blend the water and mushrooms until creamy. Add the tahini and continue blending. Add the remaining ingredients and blend until smooth.

Serving suggestions:

- Use as a gravy sauce for raw mashed cauliflower.
- Serve this on top of chopped vegetables, such as zucchini and tomatoes, to give them a gourmet experience.

Spicy Thyme Bisque

Yield 3 cups

This soup is fabulous. The first time I prepared it for my clients, every one of them told me they loved it.

> 3 cups spinach, packed
>
> 1 ½ cups water
>
> 1 mango, peeled, pitted and chopped
>
> 1 ½ tablespoons fresh lemon juice
>
> 1 teaspoon dried thyme
>
> 1 clove garlic
>
> ⅛ teaspoon cayenne pepper, or more to taste
>
> ¼ teaspoon Himalayan crystal salt, or more to taste
>
> ¼ cup raw olive oil or ½ avocado (pitted and peeled)

Blend all of the ingredients together until smooth and creamy.

Variations:

- Substitute banana for the mango.
- Reduce the calories by omitting the oil (and/or avocado) and add banana or more mango or both. Banana and mango are great for giving soups a creamy texture without adding fat. It might come across as spicier without the fat (although the additional fruit can help offset that); however, it's a safe bet to reduce the cayenne to a pinch and season to taste.

Yin-Yang Soup

Yield 2 servings

Tahini, made from ground sesame seeds, is wonderful. Sesame seeds are among the highest in being able to help lower cholesterol because of their phytosterol content. But, that's not all; they're also full of iron, potassium, manganese, copper, protein, and fiber.

1 cup young Thai coconut water

1 cup young Thai coconut meat

1 zucchini, peeled and chopped

¼ cup water

¼ cup raw tahini

1 tablespoon fresh ginger, peeled and grated

2 ½ tablespoons raw agave nectar

1 tablespoon tamari, wheat-free, or more to taste

2 tablespoons fresh lemon juice

2 tablespoons fresh lime juice

½ teaspoon chili powder

½ teaspoon ground turmeric

1 clove garlic

¼ teaspoon Himalayan crystal salt

½ cup bok choy, chopped

Combine all of the ingredients, except the bok choy, in a blender and puree until smooth, adding only as much water as you need for a creamy soup. Stir in the bok choy and serve.

Park-Side Tomato Almond Soup

Yield 4 cups

There are unique flavors in this soup, so enjoy them as they all dance at different times on your tongue. Adding the kelp is a popular version, and I definitely recommend trying it. By all means, feel free to add more kelp if you're a fan of ocean flavors.

> 4 medium tomatoes, chopped
>
> 2 tablespoons red onion
>
> ¼ cup plus 2 tablespoons raw almond butter
>
> 1 tablespoon Italian seasoning
>
> 1 tablespoon fresh lemon juice
>
> 1 teaspoon kelp, optional
>
> ¾–1 teaspoon Himalayan crystal salt, or more to taste
>
> ¼ teaspoon cayenne pepper
>
> 2 tablespoons fresh basil, chopped or 2 teaspoons dried
>
> 1 red bell pepper, seeded and diced

Combine all of the ingredients, except the basil and diced red bell pepper, in a blender until smooth. Pulse in the basil. Stir in the diced red bell pepper.

Princess Pink Strawberry Soup

See photo at KristensRaw.com/photos.

Yield approximately 2 cups

This exquisite soup brings out both the little girl and woman in me. The color is the color that little princesses wear, yet the flavor has both a light zing and delicate sweetness to it that will tantalize a slightly more grownup palate. So, get out your body glitter (for the princess in you) and your favorite high heels (for the woman in you), and enjoy this delicious creation!

¼ cup fresh orange juice

3 cups strawberries, destemmed and chopped

4 soft dates, pitted

½ (heaping) teaspoon fresh orange zest

¼ teaspoon vanilla extract

Blend all of the ingredients together until smooth.

Moroccan Rose Gazpacho

Yield 5–6 servings

This is an elegant recipe with all of the different flavors, yet so simple to make. It's a favorite of my mom's because she loves Moroccan flavors, including rose water.

3 tomatoes, chopped

1 cucumber, peeled, seeded, and chopped

⅓ cup raw olive oil

2 tablespoons fresh lemon juice

1 tablespoon raw agave nectar

2 teaspoons rose water, or more to taste

1 teaspoon Himalayan crystal salt

½ teaspoon cumin

¼ teaspoon black pepper

¼ teaspoon cinnamon

¼ teaspoon coriander

¼ cup pine nuts

¼ cup raisins

Blend all of the ingredients, except for the pine nuts and raisins, until creamy. Stir in the pine nuts and raisins.

Nutty Avocado Soup

Yield 3 cups

Avocado is filled with nutrients, fiber, and makes anything you put it in extra creamy, which also makes it satiating. This is one of those soups that will stick with you most of the day, keeping your tummy nice and happy.

> 1 large avocado, pitted and peeled
>
> 2 stalks celery, chopped
>
> 2 cups Nut/Seed Milk (see recipe, Appendix A)
>
> 2 teaspoons fresh lemon juice
>
> ½ teaspoon kelp, or more to taste
>
> ½ teaspoon dried oregano
>
> ½ teaspoon dried tarragon
>
> ½ teaspoon Himalayan crystal salt, or more to taste
>
> ¼ cup raisins
>
> black pepper, to taste

Place the avocado, celery, nut milk and lemon juice in a blender and puree. Add the kelp, oregano, tarragon and salt and blend until creamy. Stir in the raisins. Season with black pepper. Serve immediately.

Variation:

- Add a variety of fresh herbs, such as fresh basil, mint or sage.

Michigan Cherry Cream of Tomato Soup

Yield 5 cups

I was born and raised in Michigan so I wanted to make a unique recipe with cherries. But, that's not the only reason, of course. Cherries are full of some seriously powerful nutrition. This gorgeous dark red fruit is loaded with all kinds of fun "anti" compounds... anti-inflammatory, anti-aging, and anti-cancer.

> 2 medium tomatoes, chopped
>
> 2 zucchini, peeled and chopped
>
> ½ cup fresh cherries, destemmed and pitted
>
> ¼ cup Nut/Seed Milk (see recipe, Appendix A)
>
> 1 ¾ teaspoons fresh lemon juice
>
> ½ teaspoon cherry extract
>
> 1 teaspoon Himalayan crystal salt
>
> dash cayenne pepper, optional
>
> 3 tablespoons dried cherries, chopped
>
> 3 tablespoons fresh basil, chopped
>
> Black pepper, to taste

Blend all of the ingredients, except the dried cherries, basil, and black pepper, until creamy. Pulse in the dried cherries and basil. Season with black pepper, to taste.

Variation:

- If fresh cherries aren't available, you can substitute frozen (thawed) cherries

Deven's Orange-You-Glad Tomato Soup

Yield 5 cups

This soup is named after my adorable nephew who is always telling me "knock-knock" jokes. Our favorite is the joke about "orange-you-glad..." hahaha, I'm laughing even now as I write this.

> 1 pound tomatoes, chopped
>
> 2 cups fresh orange juice
>
> 1–2 cloves garlic
>
> 2 teaspoons shallots, chopped
>
> ½ teaspoon Himalayan crystal salt
>
> ½ green onion, minced (white and 1-inch of green)
>
> ¼ cup fresh basil, finely chopped
>
> black pepper, to taste

Blend all of the ingredients, except the green onion, basil, and pepper, until smooth. Pulse in the green onion and basil. Season with the black pepper. Pour into serving bowls and enjoy this high-energy soup.

Raw Plant-Based Court Bouillon

Yield approximately 1 quart

This is another great soup base to use when a vegetable stock is asked for or in place of water in other soup recipes.

> 2 tablespoons onion, chopped
>
> ⅔ cup carrot, chopped
>
> ⅔ cup celery, chopped
>
> 3 tablespoons white wine, optional
>
> 1 tablespoon Italian seasoning
>
> 3 cups water
>
> ¼ cup raw olive oil or hemp oil

In a blender place the onion, carrot, celery, wine, Italian seasoning, and 2 cups of the water. Blend until pureed. Through the top of the blender, drizzle in the raw olive oil, while the blender is running on low speed. Add the remaining cup of the water and blend. Strain the mixture through a nut milk bag.

Secret Garden Ginger Energy Soup

Yield 4 servings

1 ½ cups zucchini, chopped

1 apple, cored and chopped

3 cups spinach

1 cup water

1 avocado, pitted and peeled

1 tablespoon tamari, wheat-free

2 tablespoons fresh lime juice

2 tablespoons fresh orange juice

1 tablespoon ginger, grated

dash cinnamon

dash cayenne pepper, or more to taste

1 tablespoon fresh dill, chopped or 1 teaspoon dried

½ cup corn kernels, cut off of cob (1 ear)

½ cup carrots, diced

1 cup zucchini, spiralized

¼ cup currants (or raisins)

Blend the zucchini, apple, spinach and water in a blender until smooth. Add the avocado, tamari, lime juice, orange juice, ginger, cinnamon and cayenne and blend. Pulse in the dill. Pour into a large bowl and stir in the corn, carrots, zucchini and currants.

Savory On-the-Go Soup

See photo at KristensRaw.com/photos.

Yield approximately 3 ½ cups

This is a great soup that is perfect for taking in a glass mason jar to work. The savory flavors and texture are light, allowing the fresh taste of vegetables to shine through.

> 1 cup water
>
> 2 tomatoes, chopped
>
> 1 stalk celery, chopped
>
> 1 clove garlic
>
> 2 scallions, white parts only
>
> 2 soft dates, pitted
>
> 2 tablespoons fresh lime juice
>
> 1 tablespoon Italian seasoning
>
> 1 tablespoon light miso
>
> ¼ teaspoon black pepper
>
> 1 avocado, pitted and peeled

Blend all of the ingredients, except for the avocado, until nice and smooth. Add the avocado and blend until creamy. If you're serving this at home, in bowls, then garnish with chopped scallions (green parts).

Chilled Caribbean Mint Bisque

Yield 2–3 servings

When you sit back and sip this soup, it's going to make you feel like you are ocean side, relaxing under a beautiful palm tree and enjoying the warm sunshine.

> 2 papaya, peeled, seeded and chopped
>
> 1 mango, peeled, pitted and chopped
>
> ¾ cup young Thai coconut water
>
> 3 tablespoons fresh lime juice
>
> pinch allspice
>
> ¼ teaspoon vanilla extract
>
> ¼ cup fresh mint leaves, chopped
>
> 2 tablespoons dried pineapple, ground*

Blend all of the ingredients, except the mint and dried pineapple, in a blender until smooth and creamy. Add the fresh mint and dried pineapple and pulse briefly to mix. Enjoy this refreshing concoction!

* Grind dried pineapple in your food processor, fitted with the "S" blade.

Green Moxie Soup

Yield 5 cups

This soup offers the person enjoying it: spirit, sassiness, attitude and energy. It's packed with nutrition, chlorophyll, and flavor. If you're looking for extra protein, go hard-core, and add more hemp powder.

For those of you who are new to hemp foods, hemp is basically one word: AMAZING. Hemp is commonly referred to as a superfood because of its phenomenal nutritional value. Its amino acid profile dominates with the 8 essential amino acids (10 if you're elderly or a baby), making it a vegetarian source of "complete" protein. For more recipes and information about hemp, be sure to check out my book, *Kristen Suzanne's Ultimate Raw Vegan Hemp Recipes*.

2 cups water

1 cup fresh orange juice

½ cup hemp oil

2 cups zucchini, chopped

1 cup spinach

1 large apple, cored and chopped

3 leaves kale, destemmed and chopped

½ cup parsley

¼ cup fresh dill

2 tablespoons fresh lemon or lime juice

1 clove garlic

1 tablespoon hemp protein powder (or more)

1 ½ teaspoons onion powder

½ teaspoon Himalayan crystal salt, or more to taste

¼ teaspoon cayenne pepper (or more)

Blend all of these fabulous ingredients together until smooth. Enjoy straight out of a glass mason jar or in your favorite bowl topped with fresh sprouts.

Guacamole Soup

Yield 2 servings

I love guacamole so it only made sense to make a super creamy soup out of it. Avocado is one of the best choices for fat in your Raw diet, because it contains oleic acid (a monounsaturated omega-9 fatty acid), which can lower total cholesterol. Avocados also contain lutein, which is great for eye health.

¼ cup water (more if needed)

1 avocado, pitted and peeled

2 tablespoons fresh lime juice

1 clove garlic

1 cucumber, chopped

1 stalk celery, chopped

½ teaspoon cumin

½ teaspoon Himalayan crystal salt

¼ teaspoon chili seasoning

¼ cup cilantro, chopped and packed

1 tablespoon scallions, chopped

Blend all of the ingredients, except the cilantro and scallions, in a blender until creamy. Add the cilantro and scallions and pulse briefly to incorporate.

Variation:

- Make it a "guacamole-n-salsa" soup by stirring in some chopped tomatoes just before serving.

Garlic Lemon-Lime Bisque

See photo at KristensRaw.com/photos.

Yield approximately 6 cups

If you like garlic, you're going to love this bisque. Garlic is amazing: it's filled with antioxidants, which fight aging, cancer, heart disease, erectile dysfunction, and more. Garlic also has multiple properties including antibacterial and antiviral attributes—especially beneficial for when your immune system is not up to par.

1 cup water

¼ cup fresh lemon juice

¼ cup fresh lime juice

3 ½ cups zucchini, chopped

1 cucumber, peeled, seeded and chopped

2 celery stalks, chopped

2 cloves garlic (or more!)

1 ½ tablespoons shallot, chopped

1 tablespoon garlic powder

1 tablespoon raw agave nectar

2 teaspoons Himalayan crystal salt

1 teaspoon mustard powder

½ teaspoon coriander

¼ teaspoon cumin

pinch black pepper, more to taste

½ cup raw olive oil or hemp oil

½ cup fresh basil, chopped

Blend all of the ingredients, except the oil and fresh basil, in a blender until smooth and creamy. Then, with the blender running on low speed, add the oil. Add the chopped basil and pulse to briefly mix.

Farmer's Daughter Stew

Yield approximately 5 cups

This stew is hearty and nutritious. One of my favorite ingredients in it is the beet, which is reputed for having liver and blood purifying properties. Beets also contain folate (excellent for pregnant women) and potassium. Now, just because this soup calls for the root part of the beet does not mean that you should toss the leaves. Heck no! Those are filled with nutrition and can be added to salads, smoothies, or juiced.

3 large carrots, shredded

1 small celery root, shredded

1 medium beet, shredded

2 cups water

1 cucumber, peeled and chopped

1 teaspoon Himalayan crystal salt, more if desired

2 tablespoons fresh lemon juice

1 ½ tablespoons raw agave nectar

2 teaspoons onion powder

1 clove garlic

¼ teaspoon caraway seeds

½ cup raw olive oil or hemp oil

1 cup corn, freshly cut off the cob

black pepper, to taste

Shred the carrots, celery root, and beet in your food processor, using the shredding plate. Transfer to a large bowl and toss to briefly mix.

Put 3 cups of the shredded veggies into a blender and add the remaining ingredients, except the oil, corn, and pepper. Blend until smooth. With the blender running on low speed, add the oil. Pour the blended mixture into the bowl with the remaining shredded veggies, add the corn and stir. Season with black pepper to taste.

Alkalizing Summer Watermelon Soup

See photo at KristensRaw.com/photos.

Yield 1 serving

Anyone who knows me, knows that one of my all-time favorite raw foods is, quite simply, organic watermelon. The gorgeously pink, sweet, refreshing flesh calls my name every summer and I just can't ever seem to get enough.

Watermelon rocks my world because it's alkalizing, low-calorie, refreshing, cleansing & detoxifying, and cooling on the body (seriously, who needs air conditioning when you can eat watermelon?). Watermelon even contains lycopene, so all of you cooked tomato eaters out there searching for lycopene, eat some watermelon!

> **1 cup watermelon, diced (small)**
>
> **2 cups watermelon, chopped**
>
> **½ teaspoon fresh ginger, grated**
>
> **½ teaspoon watermelon rind, grated (or more!)**
>
> **¼ teaspoon fresh lemon zest**

Place the 1 cup of diced watermelon in your serving bowl. Blend the remaining ingredients together and pour over the diced watermelon. Garnish with additional lemon zest and grated watermelon rind, if desired.

Citrus Dill Delight Soup

See photo at KristensRaw.com/photos.

Yield approximately 5 ½ cups

This soup is pure delight. It's delicious, nourishing, and lively. I had my mom in mind when I created it because she loves celery and fresh dill. Understandably, it's become one of her favorites. In fact, every time I visit her house, she asks me to bring the ingredients so that I can make it for her.

> 1 ¾ cups water
>
> ½ bunch celery, chopped
>
> 1 large zucchini, chopped
>
> juice of 1 lime
>
> juice of 1 lemon
>
> juice of 1 orange
>
> 2 teaspoons raw agave nectar
>
> ½ teaspoon Himalayan crystal salt
>
> ⅛ teaspoon cinnamon
>
> 3 heaping tablespoons fresh dill
>
> 1 avocado, pitted and peeled

Blend all of the ingredients, except the fresh dill and avocado, until nice and smooth (this could take 30 seconds or so to ensure the celery gets processed completely). Add the dill and avocado and blend until creamy. Optional, garnish with a little fresh dill sprinkled on top.

Kitchen Sink Soups

The premise here is knowing that any fresh produce you find Raw and "leftover" in your refrigerator can pretty much be used to make a fabulous raw vegan soup. It can consist of everything but the kitchen sink—ha ha. Talk about a fun time in the kitchen! It brings me back to my days in chemistry lab—only now I don't blow anything up or set anything on fire.

Start with 1–2 cups of water, depending on how many water rich veggies and fruits you plan to use. And then start adding things... this could include garlic, herbs, zucchini, carrots, persimmons, broccoli, cucumbers, oranges, tomatoes, celery, beets, olives, ginger, lime and lemon juice, banana, apples, any or all of these things. Blend them up and taste.

The main components you want to make sure to include, if possible, would be something sour such as lemon or lime juice, something with a saltiness (for example: salt, tamari—wheat free, celery, or miso) and possibly something to give thickness, such as an oil or fat (avocado, nuts, seeds) or for a fat-free version try a fruit/veggie that lends a thicker and creamier consistency when blended such as bananas, mangos, or zucchini. Add some herbs for flavor, and maybe fresh ginger or garlic. Chopped olives, if you have on hand, would be great as well, or sun-dried tomatoes make a delicious and hearty soup.

Get creative and don't be scared. It's empowering! Start with the basics and taste as you go along... adding things until you're happy. Most importantly... don't forget to write it down! Believe me, there's nothing worse than coming up with a fabulous recipe and not writing it down.

Appendix A
• • • • • • • • • • •

Raw Basics

This "Raw Basics" appendix is a brief introduction to Raw for those who are new to the subject. It is the same in all of my recipe books.

WHY RAW?

Living the Raw vegan lifestyle has made me a more effective person... in everything I do. I get to experience pure, sustainable all-day-long energy. My body is in perfect shape and I gain strength and endurance in my exercise routine with each passing day. My relationships are the best they've ever been, because I'm happy and I love myself and my life. My headaches have ceased to exist, and my skin glows with the radiance of brand new life, which is exactly how I feel. Raw vegan is the best thing that has ever happened to me.

Whatever your passion is in life (family, business, exercise, meditation, hobbies, etc.), eating Raw vegan will take it to unbelievable new heights. Raw vegan food offers you the most amazing benefits—physically, mentally, and spiritually. It is *the* ideal choice for your food consumption if you want to become the healthiest and best "you" possible. Raw vegan food is for people who want to live longer while feeling younger. It's for people who want to feel vibrant and alive, and want to enjoy life like never before. All I ever have to say to someone is, "Just try it for yourself." It will change your life. From simple to gourmet, there's always something for everyone, and it's delicious. Come into the world of Raw with me, and experience for yourself the most amazing health *ever*.

Are you ready for your new lease on life? The time is now. Let's get started!

SOME GREAT THINGS TO KNOW BEFORE DIVING INTO THESE RECIPES

Organic Food

According to the Organic Trade Association, "Organic agricultural production benefits the environment by using earth-friendly agricultural methods and practices." Here are some facts that show why organic farming is "the way to grow."

Choosing organically grown foods is one of the most important choices we can make. According to Environmental Working Group, "The growing consensus among scientists is that small doses of some pesticides and other chemicals can cause lasting damage to human health, especially during fetal development and early childhood."

I use organic produce and products for pretty much everything when it comes to my food. There are very few exceptions, and that would be if the recipe called for something I just can't get organic such as jicama, certain seasonings, or any random ingredient that my local health food store is not able to procure from an organic grower for whatever reason.

If you think organic foods are too expensive, then start in baby steps and buy a few things at a time. Realize that you're probably going to spend less money in the long run on health problems as your health improves, and going organic is one way to facilitate that.

The more people who choose organic, the lower the prices will be in the long run. Until then, if people complain about the prices of organic produce, all I can say is, "Your health is worth it!" Personally, I'm willing to spend more on it and sacrifice other things in my life if necessary. I don't need the coolest car on the block, I want the healthiest food going into my body. I like what Alice Waters says, "Why wouldn't you want to spend most of your money on food? Food is nourishment and good health. It is the most important thing in life, really."

Vote with your dollar! Here is something I do to help further this cause and you can, too. When I eat at a restaurant I always write on the bill, "I would eat here more if you served organic food." Can you imagine what would happen if we all did this?

Bottom Line: It is essential to use organic ingredients for many reasons:

1. The health benefits—superior nutrition, reduced intake of chemicals and heavy metals and decreased exposure to carcinogens. Organic food has been shown to have up to 300% more nutrition than conventionally grown, non-organic produce. And, a very important note for pregnant women: pesticides could cross the placenta and get to the growing life inside of you. Make organics an extra priority if you are pregnant.

2. To have the very best tasting food ever—use organic ingredients! I've had people tell me in my raw food demonstration classes that they never knew vegetables tasted so good—and one of the main reasons is because I only use organic.

3. Greater variety of heirloom fruits and vegetables is the result of growing organic produce.

4. Cleaner rivers and waterways for our earth and its inhabitants, along with minimized topsoil erosion. Overall, organic farming builds up the soil better, reduces carbon dioxide from the air, and has many environmental benefits.

Going Organic on a Budget

Going organic on a budget is not impossible. Here are things to keep in mind that will help you afford it:

1. Buy in bulk. Ask the store you frequent if they'll give you a deal for buying certain foods by the case. (Just make sure it's a case of something that you can go through in a timely fashion so it doesn't go to waste). Consider this for bananas or greens especially if you drink lots of smoothies or green juice, like I do.

2. See if local neighbors, family or friends will share the price of getting cases of certain foods. When you do this, you can go beyond your local grocery store and contact great places (which deliver nationally) such as Boxed Greens (BoxedGreens.com) or Diamond Organics (DiamondOrganics.com). Maybe they'll extend a discount if your order goes above a certain amount or if you get certain foods by the case. It never hurts to ask.

3. Pay attention to organic foods that are not very expensive to buy relative to the conventional prices (bananas, for example). Load up on those.

4. Be smart when picking what you buy as organic. Some

conventionally grown foods have higher levels of pesticides than others. For those, go organic. Then, for foods that are not sprayed as much, you can go conventional. Avocados, for example, aren't sprayed too heavily so you could buy those as conventional. Here is a resource that keeps an updated list:

foodnews.org/walletguide.php

5. Buy produce that is on sale. Pay attention to which organic foods are on sale for the week and plan your menu around that. Every little bit adds up!

6. Grow your own sprouts. Load up on these for salads, soups, and smoothies. Very inexpensive. Buy the organic seeds in the bulk bins at your health food store or buy online and grow them yourself. Fun!

7. Buy organic seeds/nuts in bulk online and freeze. Nuts and seeds typically get less expensive when you order in bulk from somewhere like Sun Organic (SunOrganic.com). Take advantage of this and freeze them (they'll last the year!). Do the same with dried fruits/dates/etc. And remember, when you make a recipe that calls for expensive nuts, you can often easily replace them with a less expensive seed such as sunflower or pumpkin seeds.

8. Buy seasonally; hence, don't buy a bunch of organic berries out of season (i.e., eat more apples and bananas in the fall and winter). Also, consider buying frozen organic fruits, especially when they're on sale!

9. Be content with minimal variety from time to time. Organic spinach banana smoothies are inexpensive. You can change it up for fun by adding cinnamon one day, nutmeg another, vanilla extract yet another. Another inexpensive

meal or snack is a spinach apple smoothie. Throw in a date or some raisins for extra pizazz. It helps the budget when you make salads, smoothies, and soups with ingredients that tend to be less expensive such as carrots (year round), bananas (year round), zucchini and cucumbers (in the summer), etc.

Kristen Suzanne's Tip: A Note About Herbs

Hands down, fresh herbs taste the best and have the highest nutritional value. While I recommend fresh herbs whenever possible, you can substitute dried herbs if necessary. But do so in a ratio of:

3 parts fresh to 1 part dried

Dried herbs impart a more concentrated flavor, which is why you need less of them. For instance, if your recipe calls for three tablespoons of fresh basil, you'll be fine if you use one tablespoon of dried basil instead.

The Infamous Salt Question: What Kind Do I Use?

All life on earth began in the oceans, so it's no surprise that organisms' cellular fluids chemically resemble sea water. Saltwater in the ocean is "salty" due to many, many minerals, not just sodium chloride. We need these minerals, not coincidentally, in roughly the same proportion that they exist in... guess where?... the ocean! (You've just gotta love Mother Nature.)

So when preparing food, I always use sea salt, which can be found at any health food store. Better still is sea salt that was deposited into salt beds before the industrial revolution started spewing toxins into the world's waterways. My personal preference is Himalayan Crystal Salt, fine granules. It's mined high in the mountains from ancient sea-beds, has a beautiful pink color, and imparts more than 84 essential minerals into your diet. You can use either the Himalayan crystal variety or Celtic Sea Salt, but I would highly recommend sticking to at least one of these two. You can buy Himalayan crystal salt through KristensRaw .com/store.

Kristen Suzanne's Tip: Start Small with Strong Flavors

FLAVORS AND THEIR STRENGTH

There are certain flavors and ingredients that are particularly strong, such as garlic, ginger, onion, and salt. It's important to observe patience here, as these are flavors that can be loved or considered offensive, depending on who is eating the food. I know people who want the maximum amount of salt called for in a recipe and I know some who are highly sensitive to it. There-fore, to make the best possible Raw experience for you, I recom-mend starting on the "small end" especially with ingredients like garlic, ginger, strong savory herbs and seasonings, onions (any variety), citrus, and even salt. If I've given you a range in a rec-ipe, for instance ¼–½ *teaspoon Himalayan crystal salt* then I rec-ommend starting with the smaller amount, and then tasting it. If you don't love it, then add a little more of that ingredient and taste it again. Start small. It's worth the extra 60 seconds it might take you to do this. You might end up using less, sav-ing it for the next recipe you make and voila, you're saving a lit-tle money.

LESSON #1: It's very hard to correct any flavors of excess, so start small and build.

LESSON #2: *Write it down.* When an ingredient offers a "range" for itself, write down the amount you liked best. If you use an "optional" ingredient, make a note about that as well.

One more thing to know about some strong flavors like the ones mentioned above... with Raw food, these flavors can intensify the finished product as each day passes. For example, the garlic in your soup, on the day you made it, might be perfect. On day two, it's still really great but a little stronger in flavor. And by day three, you might want to carry around your toothbrush or a little chewing gum!

HERE IS A TIP TO HELP CONTROL THIS

If you're making a recipe in advance, such as a dressing or soup that you won't be eating until the following day or even the day after that, then hold off on adding some of the strong seasonings until the day you eat it (think garlic and ginger). Or, if you're going to make the dressing or soup in advance, use less of the strong seasoning, knowing that it might intensify on its own by the time you eat it. This isn't a huge deal because it doesn't change that dramatically, but I mention it so you won't be surprised, especially when serving a favorite dish to others.

Kristen Suzanne's Tip: Doubling Recipes

More often than not, there are certain ingredients and flavors that you don't typically double in their entirety, if you're making a double or triple batch of a recipe. These are strong-flavored ingredients similar to those mentioned above (salt, garlic, ginger, herbs, seasoning, etc). A good rule of thumb is this: For a double batch, use 1.5 times the amount for certain ingredients. Taste it and see if you need the rest. For instance, if I'm making a "double batch" of soup, and the normal recipe calls for 1 tablespoon of Himalayan crystal salt, then I'll put in 1 ½ tablespoons to start, instead of two. Then, I'll taste it and add the remaining ½ tablespoon, if necessary.

This same principle is not necessarily followed when dividing a recipe in half. Go ahead and simply divide in half, or by whatever amount you're making. If there is a range for a particular ingredient provided, I still recommend that you use the smaller amount of an ingredient when dividing. Taste the final product and then decide whether or not to add more.

My recipes provide a variety of yields, as you'll see below. Some recipes make 2 servings and some make 4–6 servings. For those of you making food for only yourself, then simply cut the recipes making 4–6 servings in half. Or, as I always do... I make the larger serving size and then I have enough food for a couple of meals. If a recipe yields 2 servings, I usually double it for the same reason.

Kristen Suzanne's Tip: Changing Produce

"But I made it exactly like this last time! Why doesn't it taste the same?"

Here is something you need to embrace when preparing Raw vegan food. Fresh produce can vary in its composition of water, and even flavor, to some degree. There are times I've made marinara sauce and, to me, it was the perfect level of sweetness in the finished product. Then, the next time I made it, you would have thought I added a smidge of sweetener. This is due to the fact that fresh Raw produce can have a slightly different taste from time to time when you make a recipe (only ever so slightly, so don't be alarmed). *Aahhh, here is the silver lining!* This means you'll never get bored living the Raw vegan lifestyle because your recipes can change a little in flavor from time to time, even though you followed the same recipe. Embrace this natural aspect of produce and love it for everything that it is.

This is much less of an issue with cooked food. Most of the water is taken out of cooked food, so you typically get the same flavors and experience each and every time. Boring!

Kristen Suzanne's Tip: Ripeness and Storage for Your Fresh Produce

1. I never use green bell peppers because they are not "ripe." This is why so many people have a hard time digesting them (often "belching" after eating them). To truly experience the greatest health, it's important to eat fruits and vegetables at their peak ripeness. Therefore, make sure you only use red, orange, or yellow bell peppers. Store these in your refrigerator.

2. A truly ripe banana has some brown freckles or spots on the peel. This is when you're supposed to eat a banana. Store these on your countertop away from other produce, because bananas give off a gas as they ripen, which will affect the ripening process of your other produce. And, if you have a lot of bananas, split them up. This will help prevent all of your bananas from ripening at once.

3. Keep avocados on the counter until they reach ripeness (when their skin is usually brown in color and if you gently squeeze it, it "gives" just a little). At this point, you can put them in the refrigerator where they'll last up to a week longer. If you keep ripe avocados on the counter, they'll only last another couple of days. Avocados, like bananas, give off a gas as they ripen, which will affect the ripening process of your other produce. Let them ripen away from your other produce. And, if you have a lot of avocados, separate them. This will help prevent all of your avocados from ripening at once.

4. Tomatoes are best stored on your counter. Do not put them in the refrigerator or they'll get a "mealy" texture.

5. Pineapple is ripe for eating when you can gently pull a leaf out of the top of it. Therefore, test your pineapple for ripeness at the store to ensure you're buying the sweetest one possible. Just pull one of the leaves out from the top. After 3 to 4 attempts on different leaves, if you can't gently take one of them out, then move on to another pineapple.

6. Stone fruits (fruits with pits, such as peaches, plums, and nectarines), bananas and avocados all continue to ripen after being picked.

7. I have produce ripening all over my house. Sounds silly maybe, but I don't want it crowded on my kitchen countertop. I move it around and turn it over daily.

For a more complete list of produce ripening tips, check out my book, *Kristen's Raw*, available at Amazon.com.

Kristen Suzanne's Tip: Proper Dehydration Techniques

Dehydrating your Raw vegan food at a low temperature is a technique that warms and dries the food while preserving its nutritional integrity. When using a dehydrator, it is recommended that you begin the dehydrating process at a temperature of 130–140 degrees F for about an hour. Then, lower the temperature to 105 degrees F for the remaining time of dehydration. Using a high temperature such as 140 degrees F, *in the initial stages of dehydration*, does not destroy the nutritional value of the food. During this initial phase, the food does the most "sweating" (releasing moisture), which cools the food. Therefore, while the temperature of the air circulating *around* the food is about 140 degrees F, the food itself is much cooler. These directions apply only when using an Excalibur Dehydrator because of their Horizontal-Airflow Drying System. Furthermore, I am happy to only recommend Excalibur dehydrators because of their first-class products and customer service. For details, visit the *Raw Kitchen Essential Tools* section of my website at KristensRaw.com/store.

MY YIELD AND SERVING AMOUNTS NOTED IN THE RECIPES

Each recipe in this book shows an approximate amount that the recipe yields (the quantity it makes). I find that "one serving" to me might be considered two servings to someone else, or vice versa. Therefore, I tried to use an "average" when listing the serving amount. Don't let that stop you from eating a two-serving dish in one sitting, if it seems like the right amount for you. It simply depends on how hungry you are.

WHAT IS THE DIFFERENCE BETWEEN CHOPPED, DICED, AND MINCED?

Chop

Chopping gives relatively uniform cuts, but doesn't need to be perfectly neat or even. You'll often be asked to chop something before putting it into a blender or food processor, which is why it doesn't have to be uniform size since it'll be getting blended or pureed.

Dice

This produces a nice cube shape, and can be different sizes, depending on which you prefer. This is great for vegetables.

Mince

This produces an even, very fine cut, typically used for fresh herbs, onions, garlic and ginger.

Julienne

This is a fancy term for long, rectangular cuts.

WHAT EQUIPMENT DO I NEED FOR MY NEW RAW FOOD KITCHEN?

I go into much more detail regarding the perfect setup for your Raw vegan kitchen in my book, *Kristen's Raw*, which is a must read for anybody who wants to learn the easy ways to succeed with living the Raw vegan lifestyle. Here are the main pieces of equipment you'll want to get you going:

1. An excellent chef's knife (6–8 inches in length—non-serrated). Of everything you do with Raw food, you'll be chopping and cutting the most, so invest in a great knife. This truly makes doing all the chopping really fun!

2. Blender

3. Food Processor (get a 7 or 10-cup or more)

4. Juicer

5. Spiralizer or Turning Slicer

6. Dehydrator—Excalibur® is the best company by far and is available at KristensRaw.com

7. Salad spinner

8. Other knives (paring, serrated)

For links to online retailers that sell my favorite kitchen tools and foods, visit KristensRaw.com/store.

SOAKING AND DEHYDRATING NUTS AND SEEDS

This is an important topic. When using nuts and seeds in Raw vegan foods, you'll find that recipes sometimes call for them to be "soaked" or "soaked and dehydrated." Here is the low-down on the importance and the difference between the two.

Why Should You Soak Your Nuts and Seeds?

Most nuts and seeds come packed by Mother Nature with enzyme inhibitors, rendering them harder to digest. These inhibitors essentially shut down the nuts' and seeds' metabolic activity, rendering them dormant—for as long as they need to be—until they detect a moisture-rich environment that's suitable for germination (e.g., rain). By soaking your nuts and seeds, you trick the nuts into "waking up," shutting off the inhibitors so that the enzymes can become active. This greatly enhances the nuts' digestibility for you and is highly recommended if you want to experience Raw vegan food in the healthiest way possible.

Even though you'll want to soak the nuts to activate their enzymes, before using them, you'll need to re-dry them and grind them down anywhere from coarse to fine (into a powder almost like flour), depending on the recipe. To dry them, you'll need a dehydrator. (If you don't own a dehydrator yet, then, if a recipe calls for "soaked and dehydrated," just skip the soaking part; you can use the nuts or seeds in the dry form that you bought them).

Drying your nuts (but not yet grinding them) is a great thing to do before storing them in the freezer or refrigerator (preferably in glass mason jars). They will last a long time and you'll always have them on hand, ready to use.

In my recipes, I use nuts and seeds that are "soaked and dehydrated" (that is, dry) unless otherwise stated in the directions as needing to be soaked (wet).

Some nuts and seeds don't have to follow the enzyme inhibitor rule; therefore, they don't need to be soaked. These are:

- Macadamia nuts
- Brazil nuts
- Pine nuts
- Hemp seeds
- Most cashews

An additional note... there are times when the recipe will call for soaking, even though it's for a type of nut or seed without enzyme inhibitors, such as Brazil nuts. The logic behind this is to help *soften* the nuts so they blend into a smoother texture, especially if you don't have a high-powered blender. This is helpful when making nut milks, soups and sauces.

Instructions for "Soaking" and "Soaking and Dehydrating" Nuts

"SOAKING"

The general rule to follow: Any nuts or seeds that require soaking can be soaked overnight (6–10 hours). Put the required amount of nuts or seeds into a bowl and add enough water to cover by about an inch or so. Set them on your counter overnight. The following morning, or 6–10 hours after you soaked them, drain and rinse them. They are now ready to eat or use in a recipe. At this point, they need to be refrigerated in an airtight container (preferably a glass mason jar) and they'll have a shelf life of about 3 days maximum. Only soak the amount you're going to need or eat, unless you plan on dehydrating them right away.

A note about flax seeds and chia seeds... these don't need to be soaked if your recipe calls for grinding them into a powder. Some recipes will call to soak the seeds in their "whole-seed" form, before making crackers and bread, because they create a very gelatinous and binding texture when soaked. You can soak flax or chia seeds in a ratio of one-part seeds to two-parts water, and they can be soaked for as short as 1 hour and up to 12 hours. At this point, they are ready to use (don't drain them). Personally, when I use flax seeds, I usually grind them and don't soak them. It's hard for your body to digest "whole" flax seeds, even if they are soaked. It's much easier for your body to assimilate the nutrients when they're ground to a flax meal.

"SOAKING AND DEHYDRATING"

Follow the same directions for soaking. Then, after draining and rinsing the nuts, spread them out on a mesh dehydrator sheet and dehydrate them at 140 degrees F for one hour. Lower the temperature to 105 degrees F and dehydrate them until they're completely dry, which can take up to 24 hours.

Please note, all nuts and seeds called for in my recipes will always be "Raw and Organic" and "Soaked and Dehydrated" unless the recipe calls for soaking.

ALMOND PULP

Some of my recipes call for "almond pulp," which is really easy to make. After making your fresh almond milk (see Nut/Seed Milk recipe, Appendix A) and straining it through a "nut milk bag," (available at NaturalZing.com or you can use a paint strainer bag from the hardware store—much cheaper), you will find a nice, soft pulp inside the bag. Turn the bag inside out and flatten the pulp out onto a ParaFlexx dehydrator sheet with a spatula or your hand. Dehydrate the pulp at 140 degrees F for one hour, then lower the temperature to 105 degrees F and continue dehydrating until the almond pulp is dry (up to 24 hours). Break the pulp into chunks and store in the freezer until you're ready to use it. Before using the almond pulp, grind it into a flour in your blender or food processor.

SOY LECITHIN

Some recipes (desserts, in particular) will call for soy lecithin, which is extracted from soybean oil. This optional ingredient is not Raw. If you use soy lecithin, I highly recommend using a brand that is "non-GMO," meaning it was processed without any genetically modified ingredients (a great brand is Health Alliance®). Soy lecithin helps your dessert (cheesecake, for example) maintain a firmer texture.

There is another lecithin option on the market, Sunflower Lecithin. This is used as an emulsifier in recipes. Soy lecithin is a common "go-to" source, but not everyone wants a soy product. That's all changed now that sunflower lecithin is available. You can find a link to purchase it at KristensRaw.com/store.

ICE CREAM FLAVORINGS

When making Raw vegan ice cream, it's better to use alcohol-free extracts so they freeze better.

SWEETENERS

The following is a list of sweeteners that you might see used in my recipes. It's important to know that the healthiest sweeteners are fresh whole fruits, including fresh dates. That said, dates sometimes compromise texture in recipes. As a chef, I look for great texture, and as a health food advocate, I lean towards fresh dates. But as a consultant helping people embrace a Raw vegan lifestyle, I'm also supportive of helping them transition, which sometimes means using raw agave nectar, or some other easy-to-use sweetener that might not have the healthiest ranking in the Raw food world, but is still much healthier than most sweeteners used in the Standard American Diet.

Most of my recipes can use pitted dates in place of raw agave nectar. There is some debate among Raw food enthusiasts as to whether agave nectar is Raw. The company I primarily use (Madhava®) claims to be Raw and says they do not heat their Raw agave nectar above 118 degrees F. If however, you still want to eat the healthiest of sweeteners, then bypass the raw agave nectar and use pitted dates. In most recipes, you can simply substitute 1–2 pitted dates for 1 tablespoon of raw agave nectar. Dates will not give you a super creamy texture, but the texture can be improved by making a "date paste" (pureeing pitted and soaked dates—with their soak water, plus some additional water, if necessary—in a food processor fitted with the "S" blade). This, of course, takes a little extra time.

If using raw agave nectar is easier and faster for you, then go ahead and use it; just be sure to buy the raw version that says they don't heat the agave above 118 degrees F. And, again, if you're looking to go as far as you can on the spectrum of health, then I recommend using pitted dates. Many of my recipes use raw agave nectar because that is most convenient for people.

Raw Agave Nectar

There are a variety of agave nectars on the market, but again, not all of them are Raw. Make sure it is labeled "Raw" on the bottle *as well as claiming that it isn't processed above 118 degrees F*. Just because the label says "Raw" does not necessarily mean it is so… do a double check and make sure it also claims "not to be heated above 118 degrees F." Agave nectar is noteworthy for having a low glycemic index.

Dates

Dates are probably the healthiest of sweeteners, because they're a fresh whole food (I'm a big fan of Medjool dates). Fresh organic dates are filled with nutrition, including calcium and magnesium. I like to call dates, "Nature's Candy."

Feel free to use dates instead of agave or honey in raw vegan recipes. If a recipe calls for ½ cup of raw agave, then you can substitute with approximately ½ cup of pitted dates (or more).

You can also make a recipe of Date Paste to replace raw agave (or to use in combination with it). It's not always as sweet as agave, so you might want to adjust the amount according to your taste by using a bit more Date Paste (see recipe, Appendix A).

Honey

Most honey is technically raw, but it is not vegan by most definitions of "vegan" because it is produced by animals, who therefore are at risk of being mistreated. While honey does not have the health risks associated with animal byproducts such as eggs or dairy, it can spike the body's natural sugar levels. Agave nectar has a lower, healthier glycemic index and can replace any recipe you find that calls for honey, in a 1 to 1 ratio.

Maple Syrup

Maple syrup is made from boiled sap of the maple tree. It is not considered raw, but some people still use it as a sweetener in certain dishes.

Rapadura®

This is a dried sugarcane juice, and it's not raw. It is, however, an unrefined and unbleached organic whole-cane sugar. It imparts a nice deep sweetness to your recipes, even if you only use a little. Feel free to omit it if you'd like to adhere to a strictly Raw program.

Stevia

This is from the leaf of the stevia plant. It has a sweet taste and doesn't elevate blood sugar levels. It's very sweet, so you'll want to use much less stevia than you would any other sweetener. My mom actually grows her own stevia. It's a great addition in fresh smoothies, for example, to add some sweetness without the calories. When possible, the best way to have stevia is grow it yourself.

Yacon Syrup

This sweetener has a low glycemic index, making it very attractive to some people. It has a molasses-type flavor that is very enjoyable. You can replace raw agave with this sweetener, but keep in mind that it's not as sweet in flavor as raw agave nectar. The brand I usually buy is Navitas Naturals, which is available at NavitasNaturals.com. For more information, see Appendix B, Resources.

SUN-DRIED TOMATOES

By far, the best sun-dried tomatoes are those you make yourself with a dehydrator. If you don't have a dehydrator, make sure you buy the "dry" sun-dried tomatoes, usually found in the bulk section of your health food market. Don't buy the kind that are packed in a jar of oil.

Also… don't buy sun-dried tomatoes if they're really dark (almost black) because these just don't taste as good. Again, I recommend making them yourself if you truly want the freshest flavor possible. It's really fun to do!

EATING WITH YOUR EYES

Most of us, if not all, naturally eat with our eyes before taking a bite of food. So, do yourself a favor and make your eating experience the best ever with the help of a simple, gorgeous presentation. Think of it this way, with real estate, it's always *location, location, location*, right? Well, with food, it's always *presentation, presentation, presentation*.

Luckily, Raw food does this on its own with all of its naturally vibrant and bright colors. But I take it even one step farther—I use my best dishes when I eat. I use my beautiful wine glasses for my smoothies and juices. I use my fancy goblets for many of my desserts. Why? Because I'm worth it. And, so are you! Don't save your good china just for company. Believe me, you'll notice the difference. Eating well is an attitude, and when you take care of yourself, your body will respond in kind.

ONLINE RESOURCES FOR GREAT PRODUCTS

For a complete and detailed list of my favorite kitchen tools, products, and various foods (all available online), please visit: KristensRaw.com/store.

BOOK & DVD RECOMMENDATIONS

I highly recommend reading the following life-changing books and DVDs.

- *Diet for a New America,* by John Robbins
- *The Food Revolution,* by John Robbins
- *The China Study,* by T. Colin Campbell
- *Skinny Bitch,* by Rory Freedman
- *Food, Inc.* (DVD)
- *Food Matters* (DVD)
- *The Future of Food* (DVD)
- *Earthlings* (DVD)

MEASUREMENT CONVERSIONS

1 tablespoon = 3 teaspoons

1 ounce = 2 tablespoons

¼ cup = 4 tablespoons

⅓ cup = 5 ⅓ tablespoons

1 cup = 8 ounces

= 16 tablespoons

= ½ pint

½ quart = 1 pint

= 2 cups

1 gallon = 4 quarts

= 8 pints

= 16 cups

= 128 ounces

Nourishing Rejuvelac

Yield 1 gallon

Rejuvelac is a cheesy-tasting liquid that is rich in enzymes and healthy flora to support a healthy intestine and digestion. Get comfortable making this super easy recipe because its use goes beyond just drinking it between meals.

Some people are concerned about the wheat aspect to wheat berries being used in most Rejuvelac recipes. While many people easily tolerate Rejuvelac made with wheat berries in spite of having wheat intolerance issues, there are other ingredients you can use to make Rejuvelac wheat-free. Some options are buckwheat, rice, quinoa, and more.

1 cup soft wheat berries, rye berries, or a mixture

water

Place the wheat berries in a half-gallon jar and fill the jar with water. Screw the lid on the jar and soak the wheat berries overnight (10–12 hours) on your counter. The next morning, drain and rinse them. Sprout the wheat berries for 2 days, draining and rinsing 1–2 times a day.

Then, fill the jar with purified water and screw on the lid, or cover with cheesecloth secured with a rubber band. Allow to ferment for 24–36 hours, or until the desired tartness is achieved. It should have a cheesy, almost tart/lemony flavor and scent.

Strain your rejuvelac into another glass jar and store in the refrigerator for up to 5–7 days. For a second batch using the same sprouted wheat berries, fill the same jar of already sprouted berries with water again, and allow to ferment for 24 hours. Strain off the rejuvelac as you did the time before this. You can do this process yet again, noting that each time the rejuvelac gets a little weaker in flavor.

Enjoy ¼–1 cup of Nourishing Rejuvelac first thing in the morning and/or between meals. It's best to start with a small amount and work your way up as your body adjusts.

Suggestion:

- For extra nutrition and incredible flavor, Nourishing Rejuvelac can be used in various recipes such as raw vegan cheeses, desserts, smoothies, soups, dressings and more. Simply use it in place of the water required by the recipe.

Date Paste

Yield 1–1 ¼ cups

It's great to keep this on hand in the refrigerator so you have it available and ready to use. Date Paste is easy to make and should take you less than 10 minutes to prepare once your dates are soaked. Store it in an airtight container in the refrigerator (a glass mason jar is perfect).

15 medjool dates, pitted, soaked 15 minutes (reserve soak water)

¼–½ cup reserved "soak water"

Using a food processor, fitted with the "S" blade, puree the ingredients until you have a smooth paste.

Crème Fraiche

Yield approximately 2 cups

1 cup raw cashews

¼–½ cup Nourishing Rejuvelac (see recipe, Appendix A)

1–2 tablespoons raw agave nectar

Place the cashews in a bowl and cover with enough water by about an inch. Let them soak for 1 hour. Drain off the water and give them a quick rinse.

Blend the ingredients until smooth. Store in an airtight glass mason jar for up to 5 days. This freezes well, so feel free to make a double batch for future use.

Nut/Seed Milk (regular)

Yield 4–5 cups

The creamiest nut/seed milk traditionally comes from hemp seeds, cashews, pine nuts, Brazil nuts or macadamia nuts, although I'm also a huge fan of milks made from walnuts, pecans, hazelnuts, almonds, sesame seeds, sunflower seeds, and pumpkin seeds.

This recipe does not include a sweetener, but when I'm in the mood for a little sweetness, I add a couple of pitted dates or a squirt of raw agave nectar. Yum!

> 1 ½ cups raw nuts or seeds
> 3 ¼ cups water
> pinch Himalayan crystal salt, optional

Place the nuts in a bowl and cover with enough water by about an inch. Let them soak for 6-8 hours (unless you're using cashews, pine nuts, Brazil nuts, or macadamia nuts, in which case you only have to soak them about an hour. Hemp seeds do not need soaking because they're very soft and easy to blend, but adjust the amount of water used in the recipe, as needed). Drain off the water and give them a quick rinse.

Blend the ingredients until smooth and deliciously creamy. For an even *extra creamy* texture, strain your nut/seed milk through a nut milk bag.

Sweet Nut/Seed Cream (thick)

Yield 2–3 cups

1 cup raw nuts or seeds

1–1 ½ cups water, more if needed

2–3 tablespoons raw agave nectar or 3–4 dates, pitted

½ teaspoon vanilla extract, optional

Place the nuts in a bowl and cover with enough water by about an inch. Let them soak for 6–8 hours (unless you're using cashews, pine nuts, Brazil nuts, or macadamia nuts, in which case you only have to soak them about an hour. Hemp seeds do not need soaking because they're very soft and easy to blend, but adjust the amount of water used in the recipe, as needed). Drain off the water and give them a quick rinse.

Blend all of the ingredients until smooth.

Raw Mustard

Yield approximately 1 cup

2 teaspoons yellow mustard seeds, soaked 1–2 hours, then
   drained

½ cup extra virgin olive oil or hemp oil

1 tablespoon dry mustard powder

1 tablespoon apple cider vinegar

1 tablespoon fresh lemon juice or lime juice

¼ cup raw agave nectar

½ teaspoon Himalayan crystal salt

¼ teaspoon turmeric

Blend all of the ingredients together until smooth. It might be
very thick, so if you want, add some water or oil to help thin it
out. Adding more oil will help reduce the "heat" if it's too spicy
for your taste.

Variation:

- "Honey" Mustard Version: Add more raw agave nectar (until you reach the desired sweetness)

My Basic Raw Mayonnaise

Yield about 2 ½ cups

People tell me all the time how much they like this recipe.

    1 cup raw cashews

    ½ teaspoon paprika

    2 cloves garlic

    1 teaspoon onion powder

    3 tablespoons fresh lemon juice

    ¼ cup extra virgin olive oil or hemp oil

    2 tablespoons parsley, chopped

    2 tablespoons water, if needed

Place the cashews in a bowl and cover with enough water by about an inch. Let them soak for 1 hour. Drain off the water and give them a quick rinse.

Blend all of the ingredients, except the parsley, until creamy. Pulse in the parsley. My Basic Raw Mayonnaise will stay fresh for up to one week in the refrigerator.

Appendix B

· · · · · · · · · · ·

Resources

The resources listed in this appendix are mostly raw, but you will also see a few items that are not raw.

BANANAS (FROZEN)

To make frozen bananas, simply peel (ripe) bananas, place them in a baggie or container, and put them in the freezer. I like to use my FoodSaver®, because it keeps the bananas from getting ice crystals on them. Having frozen bananas in your freezer at all times is a smart move. They are fantastic in smoothies, and they make a deliciously fun raw ice cream (just throw them in the food processor and puree them into a soft serve, raw vegan ice cream).

BREAD (SPROUTED)

You can buy this at the health food store. A couple of my favorite brands are *Good for Life* and *Manna Organics*.

CACAO LIQUOR (RAW)

This is the result of whole cacao beans that have been peeled and cold-pressed, which forms a paste. I use this to make a number of raw chocolate recipes. It comes in a block form and I melt it into a thick liquid using my dehydrator (or you can use a double boiler). It's bitter so I add sweetener. This is available from NavitasNaturals.com

CACAO NIBS (RAW)

These are partially ground cacao beans. They can be used in a variety of ways from toppings to raw vegan ice cream or yogurt. They add texture to shakes and smoothies, and you can make raw chocolates with them. They are available from NavitasNaturals .com and other sources online.

CAROB (RAW)

A lot of the carob you find in the store is toasted. I like to use raw carob, which has a wonderful flavor (caramel-like) and can be used in many recipes such as smoothies, nut milks, desserts, and more. There is a link for raw carob at KristensRaw.com/store.

CHIA SEEDS

These are called the "Dieter's Dream Food." Chia seeds are praised for many things including their fantastic nutrient profile, which proudly boasts iron, boron, essential fatty acids, fiber, and more. Add to that the claims that they may improve heart health, reduce blood pressure, stabilize blood sugar, help people lose weight from giving them extra stamina, energy, and curbing hunger, and you might become a fan of these little guys, too. They're superstars in my book. You can find a link for them at KristensRaw.com/store.

CHOCOLATE (CACAO) POWDER (RAW)

This is formed after the whole cacao beans have been peeled and cold-pressed. Then, the cacao oil is extracted and a powder remains. I use this in many recipes from making raw chocolate desserts to smoothies to soups to dressings and more. This is available from NavitasNaturals.com and other sources online.

COCONUT AMINOS

This is a seasoning sauce that can be used in place of tamari and namo shoyu. Available from the company, Coconut Secret, it's raw, enzymatically alive, organic, gluten-free, and soy-free. For more details, check out CoconutSecret.com. It's also available at some Whole Foods Markets.

COCONUT BUTTER OR *COCONUT SPREAD*

Coconut butter is not to be confused with plain coconut oil. Coconut butter is actually the coconut oil and coconut meat together in one jar. This can be eaten by the spoonful and it can also be used in desserts, smoothies, spreads, and more. There are two companies that I buy this from: WildernessFamilyNaturals.com offers a product they call "Coconut Spread" while Artisana calls theirs coconut butter. You can find the Artisana Coconut Butter at many health food stores including Whole Foods Market.

To make coconut butter easier (i.e., softer) to use, consider warming it in a dehydrator (at a low temperature).

DIAYA™ CHEESE

This is an amazing vegan cheese (not raw) that is taking the vegan world by storm. If you know of someone who misses artery-clogging, animal based cheese, then turn them on to this. It's soy-free, dairy-free, gluten-free, corn-free, and preservative-free. You can read more details at DaiyaFoods.com. I buy it from Whole Foods Market.

GOLDENBERRIES

These are also known as Incan Berries or Cape Gooseberries. They are basically a little dried fruit similar in shape to a raisin, and golden in color. The first time I tried these, I immediately thought, *"Move over crappy sour patch kids, it's time for something way more delish and oh-so-healthy at the same time!"* Goldenberries will throw a party in your mouth. These are available at NavitasNaturals .com

GOJI BERRIES

These little ruby colored jewels (also known as wolfberries) are a mega popular superfood because of their amazing nutrient content. They have 18 amino acids, including the 8 essential amino acids. Plus, their antioxidants are through the roof! The taste is a cross between a dried cherry and dried cranberry. I enjoy them plain and used in various recipes. My favorite source for them is Navitas Naturals (they're also available at various health food stores), and there is a link for them at KristensRaw.com/store.

GREEN POWDER(S)

Green powders are chock-full of powerful raw and alkalizing nutrition. My favorites are *Health Force Nutritionals' Vitamineral Green* and *Amazing Grass' Wheat Grass Powder*. Health Force Nutritionals also makes a green powder for pets called *Green Mush*. You will find links to these products at KristensRaw.com/store.

HEMP FOODS

Hemp is commonly referred to as a "superfood" because of its amazing nutritional value. Its amino acid profile dominates with the 8 essential amino acids (10 if you're elderly or a baby), making it a vegetarian source of "complete" protein. Manitoba Harvest is my favorite source for hemp products. I use their hemp seeds, hemp butter, hemp protein powder and hemp oil to make many delicious raw vegan recipes.

HERBAMERE™

This is an alternative to plain salt. It is a blend of sea salt and 14 organic herbs. It's a nice change of pace from plain salt. This is available on Amazon.com, other websites, and in some health food stores.

LUCUMA POWDER

Lucuma is a fun ingredient that is popular with Raw fooders. NavitasNaturals.com offers lucuma as a whole food powder, which adds a lovely sweetness to recipes with a flavor that has been described as a cross between sweet potato and maple. I love using lucuma powder in various raw recipes for smoothies, ice cream, cheesecake, nut milk, cookies, brownies, and more. There are other online sources for lucuma powder as well.

MACA POWDER

Maca is a plant that is used as a root and medicinal herb. Many people claim it gives them tons of energy and increased stamina for exercise, long workdays, and even libido! Personally, I'm not a huge fan of maca's flavor (to me, it smells like feet and tastes accordingly—haha), but this is one of the most popular superfoods among Raw vegans (so many people love it!), and for good reason with its reputed benefits. (Did I mention libido?) There is a link for maca powder at KristensRaw.com/store.

MESQUITE POWDER

This comes in a powder form that offers nutrition with a smoky, malt-like, and caramel flavor. This is available from NavitasNaturals.com and other online sources.

MISO

My all-time favorite source of organic miso is South River Miso. It's the ONLY brand I use. They have so many amazing flavors (including soy-free varieties). Check them out at SouthRiverMiso.com. Two of my favorite flavors are *Dandelion Leek* and *Garlic Red Pepper*. You can use other brands of light or dark miso in place of the fancier flavors I've used in these recipes, but South River Miso is amazing so I highly recommend it.

MULBERRIES

These are lightly sweet with a wonderful texture that makes it hard to stop eating them. I consider these delights a superfood because of their nutrient content, including a decent source of protein. They are available from NavitasNaturals.com.

NON-DAIRY (PLANT-BASED) MILK

There are plenty of plant-based milks available for purchase in various grocery stores. They are not raw, but they are vegan and many are available as organic, which I highly recommend. Here are some options: almond, hemp, rice, soy, hazelnut, oat, and coconut. Plus, there are different flavors within those varieties such as plain, vanilla, and chocolate.

NUT / SEED BUTTERS (RAW)

Raw nut butters can be bought at most health food stores or you can easily make your own (simply grind nuts with a dash of Himalayan crystal salt in a food processor, fitted with the "S" blade, until you get a nut or seed butter. You might choose to add a little olive oil to help facilitate the processing. This could take 3–8 minutes).

There are different varieties available such as hemp seed butter, almond butter, hazelnut butter, pecan butter, sunflower seed butter, pumpkin seed butter, cashew butter, walnut butter, macadamia nut butter, and more. Some excellent brands are *Living Tree Community, Rejuvenative Brands, Wilderness Poets (online)*, and *Artisana*. I usually buy them from Whole Foods Market.

OLIVES (RAW)

I truly love *Essential Living Foods'* Black Bojita Olives. They are juicy, fresh, and delicious. It's hard to stop at eating only one! They are available at Whole Foods Market and online at EssentialLivingFoods.com. I also use *Living Tree Community's* Sun-Dried Olives in some recipes. They're different in taste and texture than the Black Bojita Olives.

OLIVE OIL (RAW)

I enjoy two truly raw olive oils: *Living Tree Community* (LivingTreeCommunity.com, also available at some Whole Foods Markets) and *Wilderness Family Naturals* (available online at WildernessFamilyNaturals.com).

ORANGE PEEL POWDER

This is a powder, which is the dried, finely ground orange peel (it's where you'll find many of the orange's nutrients, too). This is available from MountainRoseHerbs.com (They also have lemon peel powder.)

PROTEIN POWDER

I use various raw vegan protein powders to get extra protein in my life. My favorites are hemp and sprouted raw brown rice protein powders.

In general, when I'm drinking the sprouted raw brown rice protein powder (by just mixing it with water), I like the chocolate and natural flavors from *Sun Warrior* or the plain flavor of *Sprout Living's EPIC Protein*. Hemp foods, *Sun Warrior* protein powder and *Sprout Living* protein powder are available at KristensRaw.com/store.

RAPADURA

This is a dried sugarcane juice, and it is not Raw. It is, however, an unrefined and unbleached organic whole-cane sugar. I buy mine at Whole Foods Market.

RIGHTEOUSLY RAW CACAO BARS (EARTH SOURCE ORGANICS)

Even though this is not an ingredient in which you'd use to make a recipe, I had to mention it here (it's an actual product for organic, raw, vegan chocolate bars). In my opinion, this is the best raw chocolate bar on the market. My favorite flavor is the Caramel Cacao but they also sell Goji, Maca, and Acai. Sometimes I just don't have time to make my own raw chocolate and sometimes I'm just plain lazy. In both cases, I run to Whole Foods Market for these (you can also buy them online direct from the company: earthsourceorganics.com). If your Whole Foods doesn't stock these... tell them to do it! Check out my blog post where I talked about my first encounter with these divine treats.

http://kristensraw.blogspot.com/2010/review-earth-source-organics.html

ROLLED OATS

I use traditional organic oats from SunOrganic.com or raw oats available at NaturalZing.com.

SAUERKRAUT (RAW, UNPASTEURIZED)

You can buy sauerkraut from the health food store or make it yourself (my favorite way). If you choose to buy it from the store, be sure to get a brand that is organic, raw, and unpasteurized. Two brands that I like are *Gold Mine Natural Foods* and *Rejuvenative Foods* (they're both great, but my overall preference is Gold Mine Natural Foods).

However, making your own is the best. It's incredibly easy and fun. For directions on making your own sauerkraut, please see my blog posts and video here:

http://kristensraw.blogspot.com/2009/07/how-to-make-sauerkraut-video-raw.html

SESAME OIL (RAW)

You can get this from RejuvenativeFoods.com.

STEVIA

Stevia is an all-natural sweetener from the stevia plant. It has a sweet taste and doesn't elevate blood sugar levels. It is very sweet, so you will want to use much less stevia than you would any other sweetener. I buy mine from Navitas Naturals (available at NavitasNaturals.com)

SUN-DRIED OLIVES

I buy the brand *Living Tree Community* at Whole Foods Market or online at LivingTreeCommunity.com.

SUNFLOWER LECITHIN

This is popular for its choline content, and it's also used as an emulsifier in recipes. Soy lecithin is a common "go-to" source for this purpose, but not everyone wants a soy product. That is all changed now that sunflower lecithin is available. I like adding it to raw soups, smoothies, desserts, and more. You can find a link for it at KristensRaw.com/store.

TEECCINO®

This is an alkaline herbal "coffee" (it's not really coffee) that my family loves since giving up regular coffee. It is available at many health food stores like Whole Foods Market. It's also available online (Amazon.com). For details about the awesomeness of this product, check out Teeccino.com.

VEGGIE BURGER

I LOVE Organic *Sunshine Burgers* veggie burgers, which I buy in the freezer department of Whole Foods Market. Check out their website at SunshineBurger.com.

WAKAME FLAKES

The wakame flakes that I use are from Navitas Naturals. Here is what they have to say about this particular product on their website at NavitasNaturals.com:

"One of the most hearty vegetables of the sea, wakame is in fact an algae that is amongst the oldest living species on Earth. This sea green has been used extensively in traditional Japanese, Chinese, and Korean cuisine as an important health food and key component of Eastern medicine for centuries. Wakame is a balanced combination of essential organic minerals including iron, calcium, and magnesium, alongside valuable trace minerals as well. Additionally, wakame is well known for its detoxifying antioxidants, Omega 3 fatty acids (in the form of Eicospentaenoic acid), and body-building vegetable proteins. Wakame also provides many vitamins like vitamin C and much of the B spectrum, and serves as an excellent source of both soluble and insoluble fiber."

Impressive, huh?

WHEAT GRASS POWDER

I use Amazing Grass' Wheat Grass Powder available at KristensRaw.com/store.

YACON SYRUP, POWDER, AND SLICES

This is an alternative sweetener offering a low glycemic index so it's commonly viewed as diabetic friendly. According to Navitas-Naturals.com (the brand I prefer for yacon products), "... *yacon tastes sweet, the sugar of inulin is not digestible and simply passes through the body. Therefore, yacon only contains about half the calories of an average sugar source. Secondly, FOS (promotes the production of healthy probiotics within the body, which can contribute to better digestion and colon health.*"

As a reader of this book, you are entitled to a 10% discount off Excalibur dehydrators and products:

Lightning Source UK Ltd.
Milton Keynes UK

176851UK00005B/10/P